Jake St. John has taken his punches, and he gives back with equal force. His book, THE 13TH ROUND, lands solidly with the poetics of vitality—a vitality that sings of comedy, horror, and, most importantly, the movement through the everyday, with all its dreams and body blows. These knocks shape us into more than the sum of our parts, keeping us fighting the good fight all the way to the grave.

–John Greiner, *Clouded Saints and Kinky Shadows*

Jake St. John writes precise, unadorned poems that move quickly to the heart of things, pulling the reader along and offering a shared humanity and some hard-won wisdom along the way. Unflinching, and dusted with grim humor. Bukowski without the bravado. A welcome balm for these times.

–William Taylor Jr., *Pretty Things To Say*

From a deep sleep on the banks of the Salmon River, Jake St. John wakes to find himself in the ring with a punch-drunk America hurtling through the cosmos toward entropy in THE 13TH ROUND. Whether digging up poems from the ground where his forebears await his arrival as they lay eternal / under changing skies – or knocking back a late night whiskey with the ghosts of Papa Hemingway and Hunter S. Thompson at a backroads dive bar - or caught in a clinch with a fierce existential loneliness on his evening commute - or cycling back to the homestead, a tangle of kids and dogs and laundry tripping up his feet—St. John's poetry chronicles a riveting phenomenology of the anthropocene.

–Maggie Cleveland, *A Complicated Piece of Machinery with Numerous Possibilities for Injury*

Go ahead, enter the ring of Jake St. John's new poems in THE 13TH ROUND. Go a few rounds with them, then a few more. Feel the jabs of honesty, body blows of incredible imagery, uppercuts of loneliness and hooks of vision as you step from his ring.

–Richard Martin, *Dear Three Pounds*

Jacques St John's poems are skinny dynamite, fuses lit with your eyes-—then KABOOM! Read them & don't forget to duck!

–Joel Dailey, editor, *Fell Swoop*

Jake St. John is a poet's poet. If you're looking for poetry slicing the page up with an economy of words, look no further. THE 13TH ROUND is a knock-out collection—rich in mood, raw in feeling. In short, it resonates. Whether your day is chaotic or quiet, take a moment—read, reflect, and let these poems hit where they matter most.

–Michele McDannold, publisher, Roadside Press

Jake St. John's words are like old friends. Anytime you pick up a book, you know it's always going to be a damn good time because not only does he tell you what you want to hear, he tells you what you need to hear. He is that moment of brilliance by a campfire's illumination. He is a friend you share beers with as he easily bares his soul. Whenever you need a friend, you need only pick up his book and read his pages. Old friends and great writers have that ability. Jake is very much both.

–John Patrick Robbins, Editor-In-Chief, *The Rye Whiskey Review*

THE 13TH ROUND by Jake St. John is quite a read! Simple and relatable poems about being young, traveling the country, waiting for love and finding all those treasures at the Goodwill. It's about living life and trying to find success in poetry and in paying the bills, but sometimes life hits you with a 1-2 combination that can land you on your ass and leaves you wondering if it's worth ever getting back up. Serious writing but with enough humor to take the edge off. More than enough poems in this book that'll have you thinking, I know how that feels. Worth picking up!

–Matt Amott, *The Memory of Her*, Co-founder, Six Ft. Swells Press

THE 13TH ROUND

poems by
Jake St. John

The 13th Round
© 2025 Jake St. John
First edition. Printed in the USA.

Six Ft. Swells Press
www.sixftswellspress.com
facebook.com/SixftSwells
Instagram: sixftswellspress

Editor: Todd Cirillo
www.toddcirillo.com

Cover Design: Julie Valin
www.selftoselfpublishing.com

Cover photo images: Matt Amott

Versions of some of these poems have previously appeared in:
The Crossroads Magazine, Empty Skull #1, Big Hammer, oddball magazine, Black Shamrock, Deuce Coupe, The Rye Whiskey Review, Capgras, Pop-Star Poetry, Elephant, The Dope Fiend Daily

ISBN: 979-8-9924864-0-7

ROUNDS

To those that came before:

"The Edge... There is no honest way to explain it because the only people who really know where it is are the ones who have gone over."

-Dr. Hunter S. Thompson

A COMPLETE KNOCKOUT

Most of us have been there, laid out on the mat, down for the count, trying to will ourselves upright and into a spectacular, highlight worthy comeback. I know that I have, many, many times. Occasionally, it happens and the motivation for it is always surprising. What goes through one's mind after the head or heart have been pummeled viciously by life, love or liquor. The other times though, the hits are so brutal that you lay there convincing yourself that a short blackout nap seems appropriate and you simply accept that the permanent damage is just something you will have to get used to from now on.

In Jake St. John's, The 13th Round, the stories and feelings he evokes provide the reader with, if not a plan, then an inspiring message, that staggering to your feet is worthwhile and the trophies come from the most ordinary of places. For Jake, these include; kids, favorite books, parental responsibilities, love, laundry, silent midnights, graveyards, childhood wiffle-ball memories, falling down stairs, or a cold beer and hot wings.

Jake is a poet who doesn't try in his poems and he doesn't need to. The poems come through clearly and effortlessly. He places his moments upon the page as if standing naked at a title bout weigh-in. They are confident, common, and complete pictures of the scene. The reader gets to know Jake and through the poems perhaps a bit more about themselves as well. These are poems you can sit ringside with, walk with, reminisce with, try to dance with, play with and get a drink with.

Above all else, Jake's poems sing like the best corner man in the business, directing us to go ahead and take the hit, duck and weave and know when to work the inside because you might as well go for the glory—a knockout is always better than winning on a technicality. And it is even sweeter when you are the one still standing.

–Todd Cirillo, poet, editor
10:47p.m. 2/25/25

•v•

SPRING

Sometime
around
6th grade,

I put
my action
figures away

collected
a bit
of courage

walked across
the schoolyard

and asked
for her
phone number

and things
never made sense
again.

CHAMPIONSHIP ROUNDS

I took
a bunch
of lefts
and rights
this week.
Never even
saw them
coming,

body shots
and hooks,
even a few
haymakers,
and lucky shots
that found my chin.

At this point,
picking myself
up off the canvas
has become
as routine
as black coffee
in the morning.

LEAVING CONNECTICUT

I haven't
worn a watch

since the summer
of 2004.

When I tossed it
onto my bed
walking out the door

in the early
pre-dawn haze.

A full tank of gas
and empty highway
ahead.

It's a long way
to California

but I got the time.

OUR WORLD SERIES

When we were kids
we played wiffleball
all summer
on my grandparents' farm.

Another Game 7
would start
each morning
we'd hit home runs
over the barnyard fence,
hall of fame catches
down the line
by the old oak tree,
or we'd strike out
as the ball
ricocheted off
the lawn chair
backstop.

We'd drink water
pumped from the well
and we'd laugh together
because life was as good
as it could be.

Then one morning,
with no warning,
there were no more
summer games,
no more home runs,
no diving catches,
stolen bases,
or laughter.

For some of us
that summer
was the closest
we'd ever come
to any sort of victory.

SOMETIMES

On days when
an unprompted sadness
creeps in

right after
your good dream
sneaks away
like a one night stand.

You're left laying there
wrapped in sorrow
staring out the window.

Until you realize,
it's raining
and you take that
as a sign—

whatever that means.

A NIGHT IN KETCHUM

I was turned around
and out of my mind
the night I found
Hemingway's grave.

In a stupor
I'd stumbled
the street
and visited every bar
still operating
that he drank in.

In one joint,
I pulled up
a stool,
ordered a cocktail,
traveled back
to 1952,
neon lights,
mixed drinks,
reliving memories
I never had.

Then, I crossed
the street
and drank beer
with a retired couple
from Massachusetts.
We watched
the Red Sox game
at Whiskey Jacques,
my namesake.
My actual birth certificate lists
Jacques St. John
as my legal name.

Anyway,
I decided
then and there
that I'd drink
a rum and coke
with Papa
anytime,

no guns though,
that's where
I'd draw the line.

LAST CALL

Loneliness
ain't the greatest
drinking buddy
but most times,
he's the only one
we got.

TAKING THE DOGS OUT

I fell down
the stairs
tonight --
again.

Feet skyward,
head upside down,
back twisted,
arms contorted
fingers outstretched
flailing for a banister
just out of reach.

The rhythm
of the falling
sounds like laughter
with each step.

The end arrives
bruised and battered
in a pile
of sneakers,
kids toys,
laundry,
and humiliation.

Laying there,
I try to think of
how to tell the story
to my friends,
once again,
realizing
none of them
will believe
I am sober

and the dogs
stand above me
offering no sympathy.
Just wondering why
we are not outside
already.

BRICK SHADOWS

The old town
don't look
the same
anymore
everyone's left,
moved on
or died.
I've read
more obituaries
than box scores
this year,
even the tavern
changed hands.
The drinks
are still poured
and the music
still plays
but it's just
a little slower
and a bit sadder
with no echoes of guitars.

MIRRORS

I asked
my unpaid
intern

what's it all about?

and he
stood there

dumbfounded
and silent

waiting
for an answer.

STAY

Don't go off
and leave me
here alone
on the shores
of night
swimming
with sharks
in a sea
of blood.

COSMIC CHARLIE GOT THE BLUES

I came through
the old town
the other day,
passed by you
under the red light
on the corner,

leather jacket
hanging off shoulders
that carry a burden of
long hair and beard
tucked below a ball cap
cursing traffic,

similar to how
you would curse me
if I was standing
next to you.

I'm heading
to pick up my kids
from school.

You're off to do
whatever it is
that you do
now.

So many seasons
have rolled away
with the wind
since our last laugh,
our conversations
grown silent,

both of us now
just waiting
for the light,
or something else,
to change.

I'M WALKING DOWN THE STREET

I'm walking
down the street
like I sometimes do,

trying not to make
eye contact with anyone,
but it's tough
when you want to see
everything around you.

So you say,

how's it going

and howdy

 or other such things,

so as not to start
a conversation

but you have to be
pleasant enough
so the folks

keep moving
along.

AFTER READING

Last night
right before
I fell asleep

a poem
screamed
in my ear

but the dream
was starting
to take hold

and the words
became pale pinpricks
in the darkness

scattering under the pillow
before
I could save them.

SHOWDOWN

Tonight,
they come
looking for blood
from all directions.
No escape
this time.

So, I let them
have it all,
every bite,
every bruise,
every last bit.

I give up
my flesh
to the wolves
of night

whose teeth
tear open wounds
like stars shining

and the moonlight bleeds
silent across
the bedroom carpet

like a crime scene.

SOUTHERN LATITUDES
for John Greiner

I'm sitting here
in the afternoon sun
reading Hunter S. Thompson
as the good doctor attempts
to flee Las Vegas.

My mind
begins to shift
and alter
as I recall the night
I met a guy,
who everyone called
the Baron,
in a Peruvian
prison cell.

And how
we were able
to produce
the right paperwork
thanks to a
well timed phone call
from our friend
at the embassy.

We were able
to cross the border
by midnight

just as
the hangman
walked slowly down
the stairs of the gallows
and untied his rope
in disappointment.

The Baron and I
crawled through
junipers and cactus,
rocks and rattlesnakes,

finally limping through
the beaten doors
of a hillside cantina,
enjoyed a bottle
and celebrated
the next chapter.

GOODWILL IS A DANGEROUS PLACE

Wandering
always off balance
from aisle to aisle
passing glassware,
electronics,
coffee mugs
and even framed
and faded
wedding photos.

Strangers'
curious eyes
seem to judge
each step
and boxes of games
with worn cardboard corners
and painted faces
that laugh at you
from the covers.

Suit jackets
hanging off
the shoulders
of plastic hangers
like dozens
of hollow businessmen
marching blindly
in step to the grave.

A homely woman
with sad green eyes
leans in towards me
cradling a porcelain figurine,
as if it were her child,

she urgently asks,
with stale breath
Is this St. Joseph?

THE 13TH ROUND

The rejection letters
and bills connect
with a flurry
of stiff right hands,
the whiskey jabs my senses,
and the day's news
delivers an uppercut.

I stagger back
to my corner
grab my pen and paper
and wait for the bell
to ring again.

THESE DAYS

I wake
sweaty and
star lit
from foggy dreams
with head on
sorrow stained pillow.

Tears of morning
weeping down
window panes
and all the suffering
of the world
is right there
on my eyelids.

So what can I do?
Brew another
cup of coffee,
watch the sun
rise up and shine
on a bunch of
other sad fools
coming and going
this way and that
and nobody knows
the score.

Just a long commute,
a traffic of souls,
holes in shoes
and newspapers
that don't exist anymore
running headlines
about our demise.

CONFESSIONAL

When I was younger
and in my college years,
weakened
and beaten
on a Sunday
morning,

a friend
pulled me from bed
and dragged me
to church.

I sat
upright
in a haze
of morning sun
that broke
through glass
as stained
as any soul
in the building.

The preacher
spun tales
of promised salvation

and perhaps
even saved
a soul or two.

Towards
the end
of his holy ramblings

my friend
leaned over
and whispered
into my bloodshot eyes

that she thought
my whole problem

with the world
was that I didn't believe
in anything
at all.

She thought
that if I believed
in something,
anything
at all,

then maybe
I wouldn't
beat myself up
so much
and might even find
a little peace.

I really thought about
what she said
as everyone shook hands,
mumbled niceties,
smiled at each other
and yet,
in the end,
as the doors split
and golden rays pierced
the shadowed pulpit,

I just didn't believe her.

RING THE BELL

Success
bleeds
in back alleys

it's drunk
on bar stools
begging
for a shot

it's taking
two punches
to give one

it's howling
at the moon
on a cloudy night

it's staggering
to your feet
when you know

the odds of getting
knocked back down
are 2 to 1

at best.

SO IT GOES

The old
don't like
the young.

The young
don't like
the old.

The poor
don't like
the rich

and the rich
don't seem
to like anyone
except the rich.

Some philosophers say
it's all cyclical
in the end.

Some even say
the game
is rigged,
the dice
are loaded,
the fight
is fixed,
the world
is burning.

So what do
you do

when you're
born to lose

and the graveyard
already has
a spot
for you.

IF IT AIN'T ONE THING, IT'S TWO
for John D. Robinson

If it ain't one thing
it's two
and it
usually is.

Some people
hate that saying
but to me,

it's a best case
scenario

because
in reality,

generally
it's three
or four
sometimes,
maybe even six

or more.

THE NIGHT IS AN EMPTY ROOM

The moon hangs over
the broken city
like a light bulb
in an interrogation room,

shadows spill out
across the floor
like confessions
pouring from a dream,

walls close in,
voices from nightmares
hurl accusations
and I'm the only suspect

without an alibi.

I GREW UP HERE

I grew up
just beyond that
stone wall
covered in moss,
and through the woods
down the hill,
and across the creek
we found the cemetery
basking on the hill
in the early
summer sun
of innocence

and there,
through the barbed wire
between those trees
and a rotted wagon wheel
is the path
that leads down
to the sandbank
where a hobo
had set up camp
for a spell
and we weren't
allowed
to play there
anymore,
but we still did.

And over there
under that small pine tree
is where
four of my dogs
and one cat
are buried....
Even me
someday.

AND YET I

I sit here,
years past
last call
where the ghosts
of my youth
once sat
huddled
at these
same tables,
writers
and politicians,
artists,
and musicians
all in drunken
conversations
about words
and the world
and now
here I am,
on a Friday afternoon
and the only thing
that's changed
are the faces
at the bar
where I now sit
finishing my burger
and my beer
before
happy hour.

AT DUSK

The sun
pulls the night
long and black
over the city
like a coroner
pulling the sheet
over the head
of a dead body.

OVER TIME

The crowd
is turning
to dust,
the microphone
has withered away,

the stage
has decayed
to nothing more
than a pile of sand,

and here you are
looking out
over that
which once
was.

CROSSROADS

Two weeks out
from the last
holiday get together,

enough for the infantry
of germs and sickness
to dig in
and become entrenched.

They attack
without warning
in the middle
of the night
stars hang heavy
over their
advance.

By morning,
my head
is a throbbing wasteland,

eyes bloodshot,
throat closed,
and lungs
in chains.

I crawl
out of bed
and prepare
for the upcoming
battle.

Which,
in the end,
I barely survive
but walk out
of the rubble

knocking on Death's door,
knowing,
the only chance

for survival
is a pint of beer
and hot wings,

at the best
dive bar
on the battlefield.

BURNING THE MIDNIGHT OIL

Flames lick the air
lashing at darkness
that falls around me
like the curtain
at a symphony
as the final notes
fade into empty corners
sharp and relentless
like Jack the Ripper's blade
seeking perpetual
pleasure
slashing the night
in two—
the alleys echo
with the cries
of the wounded.

HOLY ARE THE DAMNED

Holy are the damned,
who walk into
the fray
with a whistle,
a ham sandwich
and no hope
of survival.
Clocking in
and out
with the simple
thought
of a happy hour
that lasts
just long enough
to allow them
to forget
that tomorrow
they'll do it
all over again.

WE'VE ALL BEEN HURT BY TIME

Her boney fingers
with razor blade nails
clawing your back
memories of an old lover
leaving gnarled gashes
across the flesh
of years
peeling back
the minutes
in strips
of remorse
like watching sand
slipping through
the hourglass
and piling up
until it covers
all that remains
until we're
nothing
but seeds
in the earth,
graveyards
full of wasted
chances.

ONE MORE SATURDAY NIGHT

The clock ticks
towards dawn
like the boots
of the warden
echoing
off the cold floor
of death row.

It'll drive some
right over
the edge
but at this age
it's all just noise
and I turn on the radio
to avoid the inevitable.

I'm not flying
any white flags
today,
as the hours
pass like
exit signs
into the night.
I'll carry on
and see this
to the end

one way
or another.

EVERY MORNING

Every morning
I pass the graveyard
where grandparents,

aunts and uncles,

cousins twice
and three-times removed,

friends and enemies,

even strangers
I've never met

all lay eternal

under changing skies;
blue, black, gray

as I make
my own way
to work

beneath
a detached sun.

Who knows
what the end is

but I know
all roads lead there–

even mine.

COMMUNITY SERVICE

Every day
down at the center
slinging meals
and packing food trucks,
we'd listen to
conspiracy theories
from the guy
they called
Ponytail.

We'd unwillingly
get caught in gossip
from one of the ladies
who could still dance
and did.

I'd see Walter
shooting pool,
quietly nodding
and smiling at the folks
passing through
the front door.

I'd grab a stick
and ask him
how he was doing
and he'd laugh
and say,
*I'm still kicking
just not as high.*

He'd tell me
how he won
everyone else's
cigarettes
on an army base
taking a Russian heavyweight
to the cards
at 160 pounds.

He knocked me down
but he couldn't keep me down.

Years later,
Walter waltzed into
the liquor store
I was working at
on the other side of town.
He strolled through the door,
Hey Kid!
and grabbed a beer.

He'd just gotten out
of the hospital
and was staying
with a nephew
who drove him
to appointments.

As he walked out
the door and fell into
the passenger seat,
he raised his can my way
in an invincible toast
and called out,
I'm still kicking!

And today,
I'd like to believe
he still is.

DANCE LESSON

She was blonde
and older than me,
we were both at
a junior high school dance
standing in opposite corners
of the gymnasium
talking to friends.

She walked through
the sound activated shadows
and asked me to dance,
wide eyed and off balance
I nodded and was shoved out
and into her arms.

I stepped back and forth,
butchered her feet,
smiled awkwardly.
We danced
to an unbelievably
slow song.
I questioned her
between riffs
I thought you weren't interested?

She leaned in
close to my ear
and whispered,
I'm not but your friends don't know that.
Tell them you turned me down.

And as I climbed my stairway to heaven
and waltzed back
to the wall of questioning friends—
I did
just that.

REFLECTION

I have
a fear

of bridges
maybe

that's why
I've burned

so many.

IN MY TEENS

Stone sober
for the most part,
late nights,
early mornings
and somewhere
in between

friends with
cigar breath
and nicotine dreams
engaged in
IHOP conversations.

25 years
in between
but not far
from thought,

never knowing
where we were
or what we
were doing,

stumbling through
awkward words and pauses,
believing in
what we thought
we knew,

but everyone
goes home
needy and restless
already waiting
for the next
weekend,
searching
for an adventure
in an empty
parking lot.

THE CITY

One way chase
between raindrops,
traveling hearts,
splashing puddles,

and car horns
riding brakes
all the way home.

We're connecting
the four points of life
on the wings
of a crow,

feathers washing
down the streets
in the gutter,

playing games
of chance
with our lives.

Let's order
another round.

PERFECT

I had an epiphany
late one night
in the silence
of an empty room

it was fleeting
but for a
few seconds
it all made
sense.

SAY GOODBYE

There were
no birdsongs
this morning,

the coffee
was hot
as I stared
at the clock
on the microwave
time passed
faster than
the rain drops

that hit
the empty feeders
like drummers
improvising
a wild solo

and so
I stuffed a book
into my bag,
grabbed my keys
and began
my daily commute,

hoping the minutes
kept the rhythm
until I could find
my way back
to this chair
and finish
the song.

SPILLED LIQUOR

To be the man
you gotta beat
the man

and lately
I ain't getting
my hand raised
much at all.

I'm not
sucking eggs
like a dog
in the street

but I am
howling
at the moon
with a bone
to pick.

My shoes
have holes
in them
and the closest
thing I've got
to alligators

are the pictures
Todd Cirillo
sends me
from New Orleans.

The only thing
I'm having
a tough time
holding down

is a job.

IN THE SPIRIT

And now
Christmas spills
its reds
and greens
over America

and we hope
or pretend
that all is right
with the world

no bombs
missing
intended targets

no guns
in schools
or malls
or theaters
or anywhere else
for that matter

no poverty
for those
with bootstraps
and a dream

no fascists

only angelic smiles
of holy men
speaking kindness
and love
seeking monetary donations
and promising
the gift of salvation

all while the seasons' lights
blink shadows
off the dilapidated face
of the homeless shelter.

SUNDAY MORNING

The sun
spills sideways
through living room blinds

falls between dust
and morning air
across the carpet.

My coffee
has gone cold
again
and I can't recall
the last time
I cared.

Waiting
for a phone
that never rings
in the hum of silence
the world
runs its course.

A broken radio
plays our song
that echoes
through this
empty room.

THE PROCESS

Sometimes
the voices
in my head
will read the poem
and give me time
to copy it all down.

They leave me
feeling complete
and satisfied

but other times
the words will stop
suddenly
leaving only
an image
and no ending

and then
right before
disappearing
they'll say to me

enjoy this beautiful picture—
now go find its soul.

SOMETIMES THE BAD GUYS WIN

Sometimes
the bad guys win,

at least
that's what
it feels like.

In the end
we're just
a heartbeat
and nothing more—

money
over civility,
over blood.

We're all dust
in the end,
nothing but mud
under the raindrops

or maybe
they're tears
and if not,
they should be.

WAIT FOR THE ENCORE

The afternoon
came to a conclusion

with the sun
behind the house

throwing down
a medley of shadows

across my yard,
even the leaves

that once danced
in afternoon breeze

have taken to rest,
three birds flutter

in the silence
as I sit on the porch

pulling from a can,
listening
to the night shift
beginning its set.

IN BED

I would
write her
poems
at all hours
of the night,

these were the times
I would fight anxieties
in silence

as she slept
beside me
with a smile

that I dreamt
was for me.

KNOCKED OUT

I try
to remember
who I want
to be,

but it's tough
when the days
throw haymakers,
left crosses,
kidney shots,
and uppercuts
that make you forget

night's tiny epiphanies
that fall from the pillow
and fail to make
the standing eight count.

NOBODY'S PRIORITY

I never looked
at the moon tonight.

I had a few beers,
maybe a shot,

I read some books
in a dark room,

then I wrote this poem
in silence.

I'm nobody's priority tonight.

PARTY OF 1

Old friends
scattered
like stars
in the night.

Shadows creep
along the floor
and surround me—
a reunion of ghosts.

They take
my thoughts hostage
and extend the silence.

The song
on the record player
has long ended.

The moon beats
a slight rhythm
in the ribs
of clouds

and my glass
is as empty
as this room.

STATE OF THE UNION

Laundry hanging
out to dry,

flapping
in the breeze–

a dozen
white flags.

PLAYING THE GAME

Seems like
we're always
down one
in the bottom
of the 9th,

always needing
a knockout
going into
the 12th round,

we're running
a 2 minute offense
with 90 seconds left

but sometimes,
when it all works out,

we catch
a hail mary,
just as time expires
for the victory

and the armchair quarterbacks
say we just got lucky.

NIGHT CAP

Sometimes,
late at night
when I can't sleep
and the glasses
are empty,
I wander down
the hallway
past bedrooms,
some of them full,
some of them empty.
I trip over laundry
and navigate the stairs
and head into the garage
where I'll stand
and look out
into the night,
usually the moon
hangs over the yard,
or at least
a street light
on the far side
of the woods
breaks through.
On some nights
coyotes yip
the darkness,
other nights
owls echo
the shadows
but tonight,
there's nothing,
so I guess
I'll go back in
the house
and write a poem.

JAKE ST. JOHN lives in the woods on the edge of the Salmon River. He is the author of several collections of poetry including *Lips Leave Scars* (with Jenn Knickerbocker, Whiskey City Press, 2023), *Ring of Fog* (Holy and Intoxicated Publications, 2022), *Night Full of Diamonds* (Whiskey City Press, 2021), and *Lost City Highway* (A Jabber Publication, 2019). He is the editor of *Elephant* and is considered an original member of the New London School of Poets. His poems have appeared in print and online journals around the world.

More Six Ft. Swells Press Titles . . . .

Between Her Teeth
Mela Bust

Prince Charming
Wolfgang Carstens

Pretty Things to Say
William Taylor Jr.

Hell and High Water
Wolfgang Carstens

Arrows Go Thru Hearts
Will Staple

Perfume & Cigarettes
Madeline Levy

The Girl Who Left You
Amber Decker

Sucker's Paradise
Todd Cirillo

The Coast is Clear
Matt Amott

The Distance Between
Julie Valin

Six Ft. Swells Press

EST. 2005

After Hours Poetry

20 Years of Glasses Clinking
and Words Spilling

SixFtSwellsPress.com